PILOT PANDA SOARS TO ITALY
A CHILDREN'S TRAVEL GUIDE

Author & Illustrator
Sarah Craig Watson

NOW SC Press

Copyright © 2017 by NOW SC Press

All rights reserved. No part of this publication may be reproduced, distributed, or transmitted in any form or by any means, including photocopying, recording, or other electronic or mechanical methods, without the prior written permission of the publisher, except in the case of brief quotations embodied in critical reviews and certain other noncommercial uses permitted by copyright law. For permission requests, write to the publisher, addressed "Attention: Permissions Coordinator," via the website below.

1.888.5069-NOW

www.nowscpress.com

@nowscpress

Ordering Information:

Quantity sales. Special discounts are available on quantity purchases by corporations, associations, and others. For details, contact the publisher at the address above.

Orders by U.S. trade bookstores and wholesalers. Please contact: NOW SC Press: Tel: (888) 5069-NOW or visit www.nowscpress.com.

Printed in the United States of America

First Printing, 2017

ISBN: 978-0-9987391-5-1

DEDICATION

To my parents who gave me the gift of studying art in Italy. To my husband Steve for encouraging me to finally publish this book. And to my children Porter, Alexa, Mason, Rees and Stevie Jr. for finding joy in drawing and painting with me.

A IS ABSOLUTELY FOR ART

Italy is famous for its amazing art. The Italian word for art is very much like the English word: *arte*. Art can be paintings, sculptures or other objects created for people to look at and admire. Italy's churches, palaces, and museums are filled with so much art that it's impossible to see it all!

When you visit Italy, be sure to see Sandro Botticelli's *The Birth of Venus,* in the Uffizi Gallery in Florence. Look for Michelangelo's marble statue of *David* in the *Galleria dell'Accademia* in Florence as well. And in Milan, you should go see Leonardo da Vinci's famous painting of the *Last Supper,* which is hanging in the *Santa Maria delle Grazie* church.

The art in Italy is beautiful and famous all over the world. Which one was your favorite?

Pilot Panda's Tip for A:

Take your Adventure Journal with you into the museums and sketch pictures of the paintings and sculptures you like best.

B IS BRILLIANTLY FOR BRIDGES

There are many famous bridges in Italy. Florence's most famous one is the *Ponte Vecchio*, which means "Old Bridge." And boy is it old—it recently celebrated its 650th birthday! Many years ago, people used this bridge to visit the butcher, grocer, or blacksmith. Today people cross the bridge to little shops that sell clothing, jewelry, and leather goods.

When you are in Venice, be sure to visit *Ponte dei Sospiri* or the "Bridge of Sighs." It was named that for the sighs of prisoners who walked across it to meet their fate. Take the Doge's Palace Secret Passages Tour. You will get to see special areas like the prison cells. But don't worry, it is not scary.

Also in Venice, go to the *Ponte di Rialto*, the first bridge built to cross the Grand Canal. Today that bridge is packed with tourists and gift shops.

The Italian word for bridge is *ponte.* There are many other bridges to see in Italy. Did you see any more? Keep a list in your Adventure Journal.

Pilot Panda's Tip for B:

In your Adventure Journal, design your own bridge. What will you sell there? Food, toys, or something else?

C IS CLASSICALLY FOR CHURCHES

Some of the most famous and most beautiful buildings in Italy are churches. All Italian cities have a church, pronounced *chiesa* in Italian, as the center of the city. The *Duomo di Siena* and its extravagant zebra-striped bands of marble are a must see. The *Duomo di Milano* is the third largest church in the world. Walk on the rooftop to see 135 gargoyles and 3,400 statues up close. It's like walking on the edge of a fancy wedding cake!

The grandest and most famous church in Italy is the home of the Pope, the Vatican Palace in Vatican City, just outside of Rome. Thousands of people visit Vatican City to see the Pope's residence. While you are there, don't miss the magnificent ceiling of the Sistine Chapel. This incredible work of art was painted by Michelangelo, all while lying on his back! When you are inside the giant dome at Saint Peter's Basilica, look up, all the way up. That ceiling is 448 feet high! Almost every one of Italy's churches is home to famous works of art, so keep your eye out.

Pilot Panda's Tip for C:

In the *Duomo di Milano* look for the red lightbulb above the altar. Write down what you learn about this very special light in your Adventure Journal.

D IS DRAMATICALLY FOR THE DOLOMITES

Located in Northeast Italy is the dramatic and distinct Dolomites mountain range. Famous for its tall peaks that look like towers, this is one of the most beautiful ranges in Europe. Bordered by Austria and Switzerland, people who live in this area speak Italian, German, and their own dialect called Ladin. Known for superb skiing in the winter, the summers near Dolomite offer mountain climbing, hiking, bike riding, hang gliding, and paragliding. They even have summer tobogganing!

In Bolzano, do not miss Otzi the Iceman in the *Museo Archeologico*. He is a mummified body found in 1991 in the ice of the *Otztal Alps*. He is still kept on ice in the museum to preserve him.

Don't feel like walking? Take a cable car or ski lift to the top of the mountains to see the beautiful scenery or eat some delicious food. The local favorite is a *canederli,* a large meatball with different tasting sauces. And of course, be sure to have a little apple strudel!

Pilot Panda's Tip for D:

Otzi the Iceman had a backpack filled with tools and gadgets. Find out what they were and list them or draw pictures of them in your Adventure Journal.

sarcophagus

E IS FOR THE ECCENTRIC ETRUSCANS

The Etruscans are one of the original groups of people to inhabit Italy. Fiesole, Orvieto, and Volterra are beautiful Etruscan cities. Their religion, art, and culture largely influenced the powerful Roman culture that followed.

They were skilled artists of beautiful jewelry, pottery, and tomb paintings. One of the best, which is also considered a masterpiece, is the *Sarcophagus of the Spouses*. A sarcophagus is a stone coffin and you can see this and others like it in the *National Etruscan Museum of Villa Giulia,* in Rome. Also in Rome is the famous bronze sculpture *The Capitoline Wolf,* a telling of the ancient tale of Romulus and Remus.

From their elaborate art works and burial customs, we get a peek at how these ancient people lived a full life.

Pilot Panda's Tip for E:

Volterra has a famous artifact—a tall, thin bronze person. Find out what it was once used for. Draw a picture in your Adventure Journal.

F IS FOR FABULOUS FLORENCE

Some of the most beautiful artwork in Italy can be found in Florence, or *Firenze*, as it's pronounced in Italian. This amazing city is over 500 years old! It was founded by the Medici family. Look for their coat of arms or shield on buildings around the city and draw a picture of it in your Adventure Journal. The *Palazzo Pitti* is one of their finest palaces, where you can see many brilliant works of art. Take a walk in the ornate Boboli Gardens behind the palazzo, and have a picnic. When you are done, take a break and have some yummy gelato (which you can learn all about on the next page).

Climb the hill to Forte Belvedere for an amazing view of the city and surrounding area. Back in the heart of the city be sure to take time to visit the *Piazza della Signoria*. This huge *piazza* (which is Italian for plaza) has many impressive statues, including a copy of Michelangelo's David. Eat *al fresco* (which literally means "in the air" or outdoors) in one of the many cafes surrounding the *piazza*.

Because there are so many museums, you will only have time for a few. One of the greatest is the Uffizi Gallery, where great works by Botticelli, Leonardo, and Michelangelo can be seen. Meaning the famous artists, not the ninja turtles!

Pilot Panda's Tip for F:

You want to be sure to return to Florence, legend tells you to go to the *Mercato Nuovo* and rub the *Il Porcellino's* shiny bronze nose.

G IS FOR GLEEFUL GELATO

The most wonderful ice cream in the world is made in Italy. Called *gelato*, which means frozen. This creamy dessert comes in many wonderful flavors, and most regions have their own favorite flavor. While you are in Italy, be adventurous and try to taste as many flavors as you can. A clue to finding the best gelato shop is to look for the one with the longest line. Keep a list of your favorites in the Adventure Journal. Have lots of fun on this yummy exploration of Italy!

Here is a list of some of the best flavors:

Cioccolato al latte: Milk Chocolate

Crema: Egg Custard

Fragola: Strawberry

Lampone: Raspberry

Limone: Lemon

Pesca: Peach

Vaniglia: Vanilla

Pilot Panda's Tip for G:

Which is your favorite flavor? Draw a picture of yourself enjoying some nice cold gelato!

H IS HAPPILY FOR HOLIDAYS

The Italians celebrate many holidays or *vacanze.* One of the biggest is *Carnevale*, which takes place in the weeks before Lent. People dress up in costumes and masks, have parades, and eat lots of good food.

Easter (*Pasqua*) is very important in Italy. Many people from around the world travel to Rome for Holy Week to see the Pope. There are parades and festivities everywhere. Many Italians spend Easter Sunday with their family eating a traditional meal of lamb and eggs. Just like here at home, Italian children enjoy plenty of chocolate eggs and other sweets during this holiday. Easter Monday (*Pasquetta*) is often spent with friends having a picnic.

Christmas (*Natale*) is a magical time to visit Italy. Christmas trees, nativity scenes, wreaths, and twinkling lights are everywhere. On Christmas Eve (*la Vigillia*) people go to church and eat a light meal of fish when they get home. On Christmas Day, they dine on a really big meal of meats and pasta, and then enjoy lots of desserts. That day, children open gifts from *Babbo Natale* (their word for Santa Claus), but they often save some presents to open on Epiphany, which falls on January 6th. This is when legend says *la Befana,* an old woman looking for baby Jesus, delivers gifts to the children.

Pilot Panda's Tip for H:

In your Adventure Journal keep track of the traditions you see that are alike or different from how you celebrate. Draw how your favorite holiday would look in Italy.

I IS FOR IDYLLIC ITALY

Italy or *Italia* is a country in Southern Europe. It is a peninsula in the Mediterranean Sea that is shaped like a boot. It has 4,722 miles of coastline. Italy also has mountains, lakes, and rivers.

The largest city is the capital, Rome, which is sometimes called the Eternal City. The native language is Italian but other languages, such as German, French, and Ladin (the language of the Etruscans) are also spoken. Over 61 million people call Italy their home.

The three colors of the Italian flag represent: Green (hope), White (faith) and Red (charity). The currency in Italy used to be called the *lira* but now they use the Euro. One euro equals about 100 cents.

Pilot Panda's Tip for I:

Keep track of all the places you go to in your Adventure Journal. Circle them on the map or draw in your own locations.

Grazie
No
Per favore
Ciao
Prego
Boungiorno
Si
Arrivederci

J

J IS FOR JOYFULLY *PARLA ITALIANO*

Italian can be a really fun language! Here are some helpful words and phrases to use while on your trip.

Hello/goodbye	*Ciao*
Hello	*Boungiorno*
Goodbye	*Arrivederci*
Please	*Per favore*
Thank you	*Grazie*
Your welcome	*Prego*
Yes	*Si*
No	*No*
How much does that cost?	*Quanto Costa?*
Where is the bathroom?	*Dov'e la toilette?*

Pilot Panda's Tip for J:

Practice before you go. There are phone apps that will speak the Italian words for you to hear.

K IS KEENLY FOR KNIGHTS

Many people do not know that Italy had many knights serving the king in medieval times. A knight, or *cavaliere*, was a nobleman who served his king in battle. They rode horses, wore armor, and had some really cool weapons and amazing skills.

The armor they wore to protect their bodies was made out of metal and weighed close to 60 pounds. Try to imagine wearing something that heavy all day! If a knight was riding a warhorse he often used a long wooden pole called a lance, and he carried a sword and shield for ground battles. To practice for battles, the knights would hold frequent tournaments or contests for the king's entertainment.

Knights usually wore a coat of arms on the chest plate of their armor or on their shield to represent their family. Each symbol in this custom drawing was different and representative of some part of the family's history. Many also displayed their coat of arms on banners outside their homes.

One group of knights that originated in Italy is the *Knights Templar*, an order of knights represented in many movies about that time period. The Knights Templar were an order of monks sent to protect pilgrims on their journey to the Holy Land. Their coat of arms was a red cross on a white background, so that everyone knew who they were. In the port town of *Trani* the Knights Templar built the *Church of Ognissanti*. This beautiful building is adorned with gargoyles, lions, and griffins. Because they were such an important part of history, you can often see the coat of arms for the Knights Templar throughout Italy.

Pilot Panda's Tip for K:

In your Adventure Journal design your own family's coat of arms. Think of a symbol or animal that is special to you.

L IS FOR LOVELY LEANING TOWER OF PISA

Italy's most famous tower does not even stand up straight! It is called the Leaning Tower of Pisa, or *Torre Pendente*. It started to lean when the builders finished the 3rd story. It took about 300 years to finish building the tower because they kept trying to fix the tilt. Today the Leaning Tower of Pisa is supported by steel cables. Climb the stairs to the top, and see if you can count how many steps there are.

Close by in a little town called Collodi, is the home of the famous wooden puppet Pinocchio. *Parco di Pinocchio*, a local theme park, is a ton of fun for the whole family. Try not to get lost in the garden maze!

Pilot Panda's Tip for L:

There are other leaning buildings in Pisa. Write down their names or draw them in your Adventure Journal.

M IS FOR MARVELOUS MILAN

Milan is located in the Northwest part of Italy and because of its location, it offers activities to do in the mountains, water, or city. *Milano* is also known as one of the world's fashion capitals.

Like most cities in Italy, Milan has an amazing church, the *Duomo* (you can read more about this church on the page for the letter C). While in the city be sure to visit *Castello Sforzesco*, the former home of the Sforza family. This 15th Century home is now a cool museum with amazing displays of swords and suits of armor. You can run around and have a picnic on the duke's hunting ground, *Parco Sempione*.

Leonardo da Vinci's *The Last Supper* is hanging in the refectory of *Santa Maria delle Grazie*. This painting has survived a lot in the last few centuries—Napoleon's soldiers used it for target practice, a door fell through the bottom of the picture once, and the wall it hangs on was the only wall that survived a bombing during WWII. The painting has been restored several times and continues to be a major tourist attraction.

Go shopping in the 19th century glass covered arcade called the *Galleria Vittorio Emanuele II*. There are a lot of great restaurants here to try the city's most famous dish--*Risotto alla Milanese*, which means golden creamy rice.

Pilot Panda's Tip for M:

Take a side trip to *Lake Como* where you can enjoy water sports, play on the beach, take a funicular ride up the mountain or see a falconry display.

N IS NOTABLY FOR NAPLES

Naples or *Napoli*, is not just a city located on Italy's beautiful coastline; Naples is the birthplace of pizza. Here you will find some of the best pizza in the world.

Ancient Neapolitans had a simple lifestyle and were very poor. They needed food that was inexpensive and able to eat quickly. Pizza, or flatbreads, were topped with various toppings and sold by street vendors.

A popular pizza story dates back to 1889. On a visit to Naples, King Umberto and Queen Margherita had become tired of the fancy French food they were eating. They asked for some pizzas. The queen's favorite was cheese, tomato sauce and basil, which the chef picked because it matched the colors of the Italian flag. This type of pizza from then on was called *Pizza Margherita*.

However, Naples is not just about great pizza. There is also the *Museo Nazionale Archeologico*, one of the best archeological museums in the world. Its collection includes classical sculptures, and the finest artifacts and wall paintings from nearby Pompeii and Herculaneum.

Pilot Panda's Tip for N:

Take a tour at the *Napoli Scotteranea* (Naples Underground). This fun tour takes you through tunnels underneath Naples.

O IS OBVIOUSLY FOR OLIVE OIL

An olive, *oliva*, is the fruit of the olive tree. Italy is one of the world's largest growers of olives and producers of olive oil. Olive trees cover the rolling countryside, and it is easy to spot an olive grove because the leaves on the trees have a silvery tint. There are some olive trees that are over a thousand years old! Italy grows many varieties of olives, which have different tastes and uses in Mediterranean cuisine.

Olive oil is made by shaking the olives off of trees and onto a blanket, then crushing them with large rolling stones. This process produces olive oil. Different varieties and flavorings create a wide range of olive oils, which you can taste while you are in Italy. Also be sure to take a tour of the olive groves and the presses. Because of its health benefits, almost everything you eat in Italy, except for desserts, has a touch of olive oil.

Pilot Panda's Tip for O:

When you are out to eat in Italy, try to figure out how the chef used olives and/or olive oil in his recipe. Maybe try making up your own recipe with olives!

P IS PROUDLY FOR POMPEII

Way back in 79 A.D. (more than 1,930 years ago!), *Pompeii* was a popular vacation town and home for about 20,000 people before it was destroyed by the eruption of the volcano *Vesuvius*. Hot ash and volcanic rocks known as *lapilli* covered the city. Some people escaped, but many perished when the hot smoke and ash buried the city. The volcano acted so quickly that the burning pumice stone hardened around the buildings and people like cement.

The city was gone and forgotten until many years later when archaeologists discovered the remains of Pompeii and even more incredibly, found that almost everything in the town had been preserved. To conserve these artifacts, the archaeologists used plaster to create detailed casts that you can see today, not just in Italy, but also in some museums in the United States. To see some of these amazing artifacts be sure to visit The Forum, The House of the Faun, and the House of the Tragic Poet.

Although the eruption of Vesuvius was a tragic day for so many residents of Pompeii, the remains of the city are so well preserved that they give us a rare look at everyday life in the Roman Empire.

Pilot Panda's Tip for P:

Have your camera ready because some amazing sights are all around you in Pompeii. Draw a picture of what you think life might have been like back then, based on the artifacts you see.

Q IS FOR THE QUEENLY QUIRINALE PALACE

Located on top of the highest of The Seven Hills of Rome is the *Quirinale Palace*. It has been the summer home for popes, the palace for the king of Italy, and is now the home of the Italian president. It is the 6th largest palace in the world.

There are great views of Rome from the *piazza del Quirinale* where two huge statues named the Horse Tamers stand. Look for the former stables of the Pope, *Scuderie del Quirinale*, which is now a changing art exhibit with kids' activities and a café.

You will see a lot of Gian Lorenzo Bernini's art here. His most famous pieces are the Ecstasy of St. Teresa sculpture, the church *Sant'Andrea al Quirinale*, and the squared staircase in the *Galleria*.

Pilot Panda's Tip for Q:

Take a walk to nearby *Villa Borghese*. Is it a mythological theme park? Is it a zoo? Go find out because it's sure to be a fun trip!

R IS FOR REMARKABLE ROME

Rome, or as the Italians say *Roma*, was not built in a day and because it is such a large city (496 square miles!), you won't be able to see it in a day either. Rome is filled with churches that contain amazing works of art like Michelangelo's *Pieta*, that is in St. Peter's Basilica in Vatican City.

The most astonishing part of Rome is the ancient buildings, which date back thousands of years. The Colosseum was the site of hundreds of gladiator battles and large animal shows. This giant circular building has over 80 entrances and can hold 50,000 spectators. The events held there were spectacular—they even flooded the Colosseum once and floated small ships inside.

Nearby is the Roman Forum, once the center of Ancient Rome, which contains layers of remnants from many centuries, like parts of buildings, pottery, and other artifacts. This was because the builders kept building over the old ruins. When you walk around the forum, you will be impressed by how big these buildings are. Think about how much work it was to build these stone buildings hundreds and hundreds of years ago.

There also are many fountains in Rome, but the most famous is the *Fontana di Trevi*, the Trevi Fountain, which contains an 85-foot high statue of Neptune. Many visitors throw coins in the fountain as a wish to guarantee a trip back to Rome. Those coins are then donated to the Catholic Church.

The Pantheon is the best-preserved building in Rome. The dome on the Pantheon is the largest in the world. Look up for the circular hole at the very center. It is called an *oculus*.

Pilot Panda's Tip for R:

When you visit the Colosseum, be sure to take gladiator lessons! It's lots of fun!

S IS FOR SPLENDID SIENA

Located in Tuscany is the beautiful city *Siena*, home to some of the greatest medieval architecture. In the heart of the city is Italy's greatest square, *Piazza del Campo*. The *Piazza* is actually not a square at all, instead, it was built in a semicircle that fans outward, like a seashell.

Sienna is most famous for The *Palio di Siena*, a horse race that has taken place every year since medieval times, with part of it running through the *Piazza*. Twice a year, on July 2nd and August 16th, ten men ride bareback around the piazza three times, hoping to win the 90-second race. If the rider falls off, the horse can still win without him.

Siena is divided into different "wards," or sections, each of which is designated by an animal. It's located in the Tuscany region of Italy and was founded by the Etruscans around 500 B.C. It has become one of the most visited tourist areas in Italy because of its historical importance and beautiful sights. While you are there, be sure to see the zebra-striped *Duomo* and the *Torre del Mangia*. Climb the steps of this tall skinny bell tower and read the time on the sundial below.

Pilot Panda's Tip for S:

There are many *Contrada* flags flying around the city. Each district has one. Draw some of your favorites in your Adventure Journal. Or design your own. Or draw a picture of you on your horse, about to start the 90-second race.

T IS FOR TERRIFIC TUSCANY

Well-known for its amazing churches and museums. Tuscany has even more to offer the Italian traveler. Here are a few smaller Tuscan towns worth visiting:

Lucca: Renaissance walls that are wide enough to walk and bike on surround the small town of Lucca. The unusual *Torre dei Guinigi* is a sight to see. When you visit it, try to figure out what is at the top of this unique tower.

San Gimignano: The astounding town of San Gimignano is not to be missed. This town of medieval skyscrapers or towers is pedestrian only, meaning there are no cars and everybody walks to get to their destinations. There were 72 towers here once, count and draw how many you see today.

Pitigliano: The Etruscan town of Pitigliano is off the beaten path but well worth the journey. This ancient city is as deep as it is wide and has many underground tunnels called the *Vie Cave*. Be an archeologist for the day and explore this unique city and draw what you see in these tunnels in your Adventure Journal.

Pilot Panda's Tip for T:

If you visit the San Gimignano 1300 Museum you can see a ceramic scale model of the city as it was in Medieval times.

U IS FOR UNBELIEVABLE UMBRIA

Located between Rome and Florence is the region of Umbria. *Assisi* is a great example of a medieval city nestled in the hilly countryside.

It's most famous resident and what brings many visitors, is St. Francis, the patron saint of animals. He was born here into a rich family and died a deeply loved monk. You can visit his tomb in the *Basilica di San Francesco*. He died in 1226, but his tomb was not discovered until 1818. See if you can find out why. His life is depicted in 28 painted panels, the *Life of St. Francis*, thought to be painted by Giotto.

Climb the hill up to *Rocca Maggiore* to run around and explore the ramps and walls of this mighty fortress.

Travel to the beautiful capital of Umbria, *Perugia*. There are Etruscan artifacts here like the Arch of Augustus, but the best part of this town is the delicious *Baci* chocolate. *Baci* means kisses. Look inside the wrapper for a secret message.

Pilot Panda's Tip for U:

For the brave souls who do not mind heights, go to Gubbio and ride the funicular. It is unbelievable!

V IS VIVIDLY FOR VENICE

Venice, or *Venezia*, is one of the most interesting and beautiful cities in the world. Built on more than 100 small islands in a lagoon in the Adriatic Sea, Venice is a cozy city where almost everyone travels by water or on foot.

In the heart of the city is the *Palazzo di San Marco*, where there are plenty of shops and restaurants to enjoy. There are so many pigeons there and it is quite fun to see the big flocks take flight or strut through the plaza. If you stand really still they might sit on your shoulders!

At the eastern end of the piazza is The *Basilica di San Marco*, an ornate cathedral covered in 8,000 square meters of mosaics depicting scenes from the New Testament. Walk up the small stairway to see a spectacular view of the Grand Canal and visit the city's enormous bronze horses. These horses have an interesting past and reason for being in Venice. See if you can find out where they originally came from.

If you like art, Venice is also a great city for seeing incredible works. There are many museums to visit, but the Peggy Guggenheim has a great collection of modern artists like Picasso.

Be sure to take a gondola ride through Venice. It's also fun to catch a *vaporetto*, also known as a water taxi, to the church of *Santa Maria della Salute.* Picnic on the dramatic steps that rise out of the water and lead up to the church.

Pilot Panda's Tip for V:

Take a tour of the *Museo Storico Navale*, Naval Museum. There you will see many types of boats, cannons, and a gondola workshop. Create your own gondola or vessel for navigating the waterways of Venice.

W IS FOR WORLDLY WINE

Italy is famous for many things and wine or *vino* is one of them. The country is one of the world's largest producers of wine and is filled with vineyards! The Etruscans and the Greeks were the first to make wine in Italy, but the Romans were the ones to introduce wine in barrels and bottles.

The Chianti region is one of the most famous wine-producing regions and the rolling countryside is covered with picturesque vineyards. Many wines are named after the region they come from, like Chianti, which is often served in a wide bottomed bottle enclosed in a straw basket called a *fiasco*. *Chianti Classico* is one of the most popular kinds of wine you will see in Italy.

When they are ready to be harvested, the grapes are picked from the vine and are crushed to make the wine. Today, machines are used to press the juice out of the grapes, but many years ago people climbed into giant containers and stomped them with their feet! You can take a tour of these vineyards and kids, you can taste some delicious grape juice. Does it taste like the juice you drink at home?

Pilot Panda's Tip for W:

Look for the black rooster on the wine bottles in the Chianti Region and ask someone why they chose a rooster.

X IS FOR X-RAY ASTRONOMY

Italian *Riccardo Giacconi,* who was from Genoa, developed x-ray astronomy, by observing the x-rays emitted from cosmic sources. He won the Nobel Prize for Physics with two other scientists for research that helped lay the foundations for x-ray astronomy.

Another famous Italian astronomer is *Galileo Galilei*. Galileo was also a physicist, mathematician, philosopher, and inventor. Some of his inventions that are still in use today include the compass, the thermometer, and the telescope. When you are in Florence, go to the *Museo Galileo* to see lots of cool scientific stuff. The telescope that Galileo used to identify Jupiter's moons is there.

Pilot Panda's Tip for X:

There are many interesting planetariums to see, but the biggest one is located in Milan. At that planetarium, you can see a cool movie about the sky and learn a lot about the stars.

Y IS FOR WHY IS THERE NO Y

There are 21 letters in the Italian *alfabeto*. The English alphabet has 26. The Italian language, however, does not use the letters j, k, w, x, and y. Here's a chart to help you with the basics of the Italian alphabet.

Letter	Name	Pronounced	Words
A	*A*	Ah	Albero (Tree)
B	*Bi*	Bee	Banana
C	*Ci*	Chee	Cane (Dog)
D	*Di*	Dee	Delfino (Dolphin)
E	*E*	Ay	Eletante (Elephant)
F	*Effe*	EHF-fay	Fiore (Flower)
G	*Gi*	Gee	Gatto (Cat)
H	*Acca*	AHK-kah	Hamburger
I	*I*	Ee	Isla (Island)
L	*Elle*	Ehl-ay	Luna (Moon)
M	*Emme*	EHM-may	Mela (Apple)
N	*Enne*	EHN-nay	Nibbio (Kite)
O	*O*	O	Ombrello (Umbrella)
P	*Pi*	Pee	Palla (Ball)
Q	*Qu*	Koo	Quadro (Painting)
R	*Erre*	EHR-ray	Rana (Frog)
S	*Esse*	EHS-say	Sole (Sun)
T	*Ti*	Tee	Tavolo (Table)
U	*U*	Oo	Uva (Grapes)
V	*Vu*	Voo	Verde (Green)
Z	*Zeta*	TSAY-Tah	Zucca (Pumpkin)

Pilot Panda's Tip for Y:

Practice the alphabet and you will be able to read some Italian words on your trip. Pilot Panda wants to see if you can find all the pictures that match the Italian name.

Z IS FOR ZESTY ZABAGLIONE

Italy is known for its delicious foods, especially desserts. There are so many wonderful choices, from the *gelato* we learned about with letter G, to the delicious choices mentioned here. Try several and see which one is your favorite.

Zabaglione is a frothy custard-like mixture of eggs, sugar and either Marsala wine or espresso. It can be served hot or cold. Which way do you like it?

Cannolis are Sicilian pastry circles that have been rolled around a tube and fried. They are then filled with something sweet like fruit, cream, or ricotta cheese and then topped with chocolate chips. There are many varieties of cannolis, so you should be able to find one you like. Yum!

Panna Cotta means cooked cream. This dessert jiggles! It is best served with fruit, caramel, or chocolate sauce.

Tiramisu is probably the most famous dessert in Italy, besides gelato. In Italian, tiramisu means "pull me up," probably because this dish has a lot of espresso in it. This chilled sweet treat is made with ladyfinger cookies dipped in coffee, layered between sweetened mascarpone cheese and cream. If you don't like coffee, other kinds are made with strawberries or lemon sauce. *Mangia!*

Pilot Panda's Tip for Z:

Draw a picture of your favorite Italian dessert, or invent your own!

CONNECT WITH PILOT PANDA!

Share your favorite photo or sketch
from your Adventure Journal!

- Facebook: www.Facebook.com/PilotPandaSeries
- Twitter: @PilotPanda
- Instagram: @PilotPanda

#PilotPanda

ABOUT THE AUTHOR

SARAH CRAIG WATSON

Sarah Craig Watson is a wife, mother, sister, aunt and now an author/illustrator. A native Floridian, she is the mother of five children, ages sixteen to three. Her late mother instilled a love of travel and art in Sarah, which led to her finishing her Bachelor's Degree in Art Education by studying art in Florence, Italy. While working towards her Masters in Elementary Education she wrote and illustrated her first book, Pilot Panda Soars To Italy, part of an all-new series for children interested in learning about the world.

www.ingramcontent.com/pod-product-compliance
Lightning Source LLC
Chambersburg PA
CBHW080415300426
44113CB00015B/2526